DIESEL DECADE
THE 1980s

R O G E R   S I V I T E R

A R P S

SUTTON PUBLISHING

First published in 2006 by
Sutton Publishing Limited · Phoenix Mill
Thrupp · Stroud · Gloucestershire · GL5 2BU

British Library Cataloguing in Publication Data
A catalogue record for this book is available from the British Library.

ISBN 0-7509-4340-8

A classic scene at London's Kings Cross station, taken on Saturday 20 June 1981. In the foreground is
Class 55 Deltic locomotive No. 55015 *Tulyar* with a train from York that arrived at the terminus at
13.45. Beyond No. 55015 is another Deltic locomotive, No. 55009 *Alycidon*, with an earlier arrival from
York at 13.10. Beyond the Deltics is a High Speed Train (HST) unit with an arrival from the north-east.

Typeset in 10/12 pt Palatino.
Typesetting and origination by
Sutton Publishing Limited.
Printed and bound in England by
J.H. Haynes & Co. Ltd, Sparkford.

Contents

A pair of Metropolitan-Cammell Class 101 two-car units head across the Knucklas Viaduct on the Central Wales line with the 15.39 Shrewsbury to Swansea service on 12 August 1983. The Class 101 units were the largest fleet of diesel multiple units (DMUs) operating on British Rail (BR). They were built between 1956 and 1960, and some examples lasted well into the new millennium. Some of these units can now be seen at work on the preserved lines.

Introduction

In many ways, the 1980s were the 'Golden Age' of diesel locomotive-hauled trains on British Rail, almost mirroring (certainly on the main line) the 1950s, when steam traction more or less reigned supreme. However, for the many railway enthusiasts born from the late 1950s onwards, travel behind steam traction was a somewhat faint and distant memory, now well supplanted by the thought of seeing and riding behind Deltics and Class 40 locomotives, to name but two of the popular classes which still operated in the early 1980s.

Although the Deltics finished at the beginning of 1982, many popular classes would carry on for most of – or throughout – the decade, making the 1980s the Indian summer of many of the first generation of British diesel locomotive classes. These included (apart from the Deltics and Class 40s) the Class 45s and Class 46s, and some of the Type 2 diesels, notably the Class 25s and Class 27s; and also the Type 4 Class 50s, the last examples of this attractive class working until the early 1990s. Most of the locomotives were to be found in the BR blue livery, which is now very popular with enthusiasts.

Although great changes took place during the 1960s' Beeching era, these were – with a few exceptions – mainly concerned with the wholesale closure of branch lines. Thus, by the 1980s, as you will see in the book, we still had a great deal of infrastructure left to remind us of the past. However, from the middle of the decade onwards, resignalling would take place and many areas would be electrified, notably the East Coast Main Line (ECML) and East Anglia. And so the aim of this book is to show this historic period through a series of photographic essays. In doing this, I must thank my wife Christina for much help, and my publisher for allowing me a free hand, but most of all the professional railwaymen who make it all possible.

Note: Unless stated otherwise, all the photographs were taken by the author.

Roger Siviter ARPS
Evesham, 2006

On 18 August 1984 the 14.45 Plymouth to Leeds parcels train heads down the 1 in 66 of Rattery Bank (just south-west of Totnes) with an unidentified Class 45 (believed to be No. 45022 *Lytham St Anne's*) in charge.

Chapter One

Class 40s at Work

This first chapter shows the popular English Electric Class 40 locomotives at work in the 1980s. These Type 4 diesels, of which 200 examples were built, were first introduced in 1958, and lasted until the mid-1980s. Several examples have been preserved and can be seen at work on preserved lines. No. 40145, which is owned by the Class Forty Preservation Society, can be seen working charter trains on the main line.

On 24 May 1981 Class 40 No. 40117 is seen heading south out of York station with an evening train bound for Manchester and Liverpool. In the background, Class 55 Deltic No. 55007 waits to leave with the 19.10 service from York to Kings Cross. (See photograph on pages 36 and 37.)

The Class 40s were to be found at work on many parts of the BR system, but one of their last regular haunts was probably between Manchester, Chester and the North Wales coast route to Holyhead, hauling both passenger and freight services.

Class 40 No. 40181 heads out of Rhyl *(top)* with the 11.35 Manchester Victoria to Bangor train on 6 July 1983. This train originated at Scarborough, leaving the famous Yorkshire seaside resort at 08.50. Note the tall London North Western Railway (LNWR) Rhyl No. 2 signal-box and the busy market on the left-hand side, and also the former bay platform where the rails have recently been taken up.

Later on 6 July 1983 *(left)* No. 40181 is seen approaching Rhyl with the 17.10 Bangor to Manchester and York train. At the rear of the train can be seen Class 47 No. 47537 waiting to enter Rhyl station with the empty coaching stock (ECS) of a returning excursion train.

Flanked by old and new signals, and with the imposing Chester No. 2 signal-box in the background, Class 40 No. 40008 pulls out of Chester General station with a North Wales to Crewe train on the wet afternoon of Saturday 5 June 1982. The lines to the left of the signal-box run to Manchester Victoria via Warrington Bank Quay and Earlstown.

No. 40057 prepares to pull out of Manchester Victoria station on 29 January 1983 with the 15.15 train to Bangor. On the right-hand side a Derby-built DMU waits to leave with a local service. This famous old Lancashire & Yorkshire Railway (L&YR) station, which was modernised and virtually rebuilt by the mid-1990s, was opened in 1844, and from the late 1920s was connected to Manchester Exchange station (which closed in 1969) by the famous platform 11, which at 2,194ft was once the longest platform in the UK.

As mentioned on page 8, the English
Electric Class 40s were to be found on
many parts of the BR system including
Scotland, particularly in their latter
days, on the Edinburgh to Aberdeen
route via the Forth and Tay bridges
and Dundee. On Saturday 6 September
1980 an unidentified member of the
class is seen crossing over the southerly
brick-built viaduct at Montrose with an
afternoon Aberdeen to Edinburgh train.
There are two viaducts at Montrose,
which cross over the Montrose Basin
where it runs into the North Sea, the
other viaduct just north of this location
being of metal construction.

For many years, until their demise in the mid-1980s, the Class 40 locomotives could be seen at work on the
former Midland Railway Settle to Carlisle route (S&C) between Leeds and Carlisle, hauling both freight and
passenger trains. On a misty Sunday 1 May 1983 No. 40029 heads south off the Ribblehead, or Batty Moss,
Viaduct with a Newcastle to Manchester (Red Bank) parcels train. This impressive viaduct is 440yd long and
has twenty-four spans.

The morning of Sunday 30 January 1983 sees No. 40080 pausing near Carlisle Upperby depot with a southbound ballast train. This depot (and also carriage sidings) is situated on the east side of the West Coast Main Line (WCML) to Penrith, south of Carlisle station. Most if not all diesel locomotives acquired nicknames (in some cases two or three), the Class 40s being known as 'Whistlers' because of their distinctive engine sound, especially when, as in this photograph, they are 'idling'.

Another S&C scene, this time at Appleby station on the northern section of this famous line. Class 40 No. 40122/D200 enters Appleby station with the 10.40 Carlisle to Leeds train on 17 August 1983. At this spot behind the train is the junction for the branch line to Warcop, which was originally part of the old North Eastern route to Kirkby Stephen and the north-east of England. Note that at this time No. 40122 was also numbered D200. The numbering of this class was Nos D200 to D399 when they were first introduced in 1958, and at the time several of the class were named after ocean liners.

A wintry scene some 200 miles or so to the south of Carlisle, near Droitwich Spa in the heart of Worcestershire. Class 40 No. 40060 approaches Droitwich station at midday on 16 January 1985 with a northbound mixed goods train from Gloucester to Bescot (Walsall), via Stourbridge Junction.

According to my records, this was the last time I saw a 'Whistler' at work on BR. The next occasion was to be on 22 May 2004, when preserved Class 40 No. 40145 ran on the 'Western Whistler' from Crewe to Plymouth, one of its first trips back on the main line after preservation by the Class Forty Preservation Society – a gap of almost twenty years.

We are still in the West Midlands, only this time at Langley (Rood End), to the west of Birmingham on the Birmingham Snow Hill to Stourbridge Junction line, on 18 January 1984. The train is a freightliner service, and Class 40 locomotive No. 40195 on reaching Stourbridge Junction will reverse and then head north with the train to Wolverhampton, running via Dudley and Walsall.

It is a sunny day as No. 40172 heads through the outskirts of Chester on 13 July 1983 with a train of empty hopper wagons, probably bound for the quarry at Penmaenmawr, just over 5 miles west of Llandudno Junction on the North Wales coast route. The train is about to cross the famous 'Roodee' viaduct over the River Dee. It runs beside Chester racecourse, which can be seen in the middle distance. Also, as can be seen, this section of track (down to Saltney Junction, where the North Wales line leaves the former Great Western Railway route to Shrewsbury and Paddington) was at one time a four-track section. This was the case until about 1980.

No. 40047 approaches Abergele station with the 14.40 Amlwch to Llandudno Junction tank train on 6 July 1983. Amlwch is the terminus of a branch line (now freight only) on the island of Anglesey, which leaves the former London Midland Scottish (LMS) North Wales main line at Gaerwen Junction on the eastern side of Anglesey, just to the west of the Britannia Bridge.

As it became obvious that the Class 40s were nearing the end of their working lives, they were soon in demand to work on enthusiasts' special charter trains. This scene, taken on 28 December 1983, shows No. 40122/D200 at Carnforth East Junction with a special train to Hellifield.

On 7 April 1984 No. 40122/D200 was on special duty on the S&C. The lonely outpost on this misty day is Blea Moor Sidings, and the train is the first section from Stafford to Carlisle of the 'Knotty Northern Circular'. On the right-hand side is a Brush Class 31 locomotive on standby duty.

The photographs above were taken on Monday 28 May 1984 and show 'The Devonian' special train from Preston to Paignton and return. The first view *(top)* shows the special (which left Preston at 06.30) as it pulls through Newton Abbot at lunchtime on that misty day, complete with many 'arm wavers' and a fair number of enthusiasts on the platform. Note the abundance of signals, sidings and railway buildings, most of which would have disappeared by 1987. This special was hauled by Class 40 Nos 40051 and 40135, an uncommon sight in the West Country.

The return special *(above)*, this time with No. 40135 leading, is seen leaving the Paignton line at Aller Junction, the line to Plymouth swinging away on the right-hand side. Note also the signal-box and the allotments, and once again the 'arm wavers'.

Also note in these photographs the front-end designs of the two locomotives. There were several different front-end designs on this class (see photographs overleaf), as well as on a number of other classes, notably the English Electric Class 37s.

We finish this section on the Class 40s at work appropriately on the North Wales main line. Both these photographs were taken on Saturday 4 June 1983, and show No. 40158 *(above)* as it heads under the impressive signal gantry just to the east of Rhyl station with a morning Holyhead to Trafford Park freightliner train. The goods shed on the left and the gantry have now disappeared.

The second scene shows Class 40 No. 40168 as it heads westwards and passes the former LNWR signal-box at Abergele with a freightliner train from Trafford Park bound for Holyhead. Note the variation in the front end panel designs.

Chapter Two
Landscapes

The line which threads the English and Welsh border between Chester and Newport is known as the Welsh Marches route, and runs through some delightful countryside. In the early 1980s, most of the passenger workings were in the hands of the Type 3 Class 33 locomotives built by the Birmingham Railway Carriage and Wagon Company Ltd between 1960 and 1962. On 13 June 1981 Class 33 No. 33002 runs through some lovely scenery at All Stretton, just to the north of the charming resort of Church Stretton, with a midday Crewe to Cardiff train.

The Settle to Carlisle route is one of the most scenic lines in the country, as I hope these four photographs will testify. The first scene *(above)*, taken from the disused signal-box at Dent on 21 April 1984, shows Peak Class 45/1 No. 45132 as it heads north with a Leicester to Carlisle special charter train. Within a few yards it will run through Dent station which, at an elevation of 1,155ft, is the highest in England. Note also the snow fences on the left and, in the mist on the right, Arten Gill Viaduct.

This second view at Dent shows Class 45 No. 45019 entering the station with an afternoon Carlisle to Nottingham train on 28 March 1981. It is just passing under the bridge which carries the famous coal road to Garsdale station. Note also the signal-post but no arm, the signal-box at Dent having closed the previous year. A few hundred yards to the rear of the train is the entrance to the 1,213-yd long Rise Hill Tunnel.

On Saturday 2 April 1983 WCML trains were diverted via the S&C route. One such train was the 10.10 Glasgow to Euston 'The Royal Scot', seen here approaching the summit of the climb from Kirkby Stephen at Ais Gill. In charge of the train is Class 40 No. 40152, and dominating the background is Wild Boar Fell, still with some snow on its upper reaches.

This scene on the S&C line was taken on 23 August 1986. By this date the Brush Type 4 Class 47s had taken over from the Class 40s and 45s, and No. 47524 of this ubiquitous class is seen emerging into the sunshine from the north end of Blea Moor Tunnel (2,629yd long), near Dent Head. The train is the 09.01 Leeds to Carlisle, arriving in the Roman city at 11.35, a journey of 112¾ miles over this famous Midland Railway route.

The photographs above and opposite illustrate the industrial landscape. Here, Peak Class 45/1 No. 45134 hurries past the well-known Hallenbeagle engine house at Scorrier with the 09.18 Penzance to Birmingham New Street train on 31 August 1984. This location, just north of Redruth, is the start of the former tin-mining area around Redruth and Camborne.

This industrial scene was photographed just east of Middlesbrough on 17 August 1986. It shows a pair of Metropolitan-Cammell Class 101 two-car units heading for the coastal resort of Saltburn with the 10.27 service from Bishop Auckland via Darlington and Middlesbrough. Dominating the background is the unique Newport transporter bridge.

Our final industrial scene was taken at Burngullow, just west of St Austell, on the former GWR Cornish main line from Plymouth to Penzance on 6 September 1985. On the right, Class 45 No. 45003 tops the climb from St Austell with the 07.50 Bristol to Penzance service, while Class 37 No. 37308 is about to enter the sidings by the Blackpool clay driers, which are part of English China Clays Ltd (ECC), with a train from Drinnick Mill. The junction for this is situated just behind the photographer. In the autumn of 1986 the main line from Burngullow to Probus (6 miles west) was singled, but it is now double track again: the doubling took place at the end of 2004. Note the rows of hooded china clay wagons in the sidings.

The Kyle of Lochalsh line between Dingwall and Kyle is noted for its scenery – weather permitting. On 31 July 1989 Class 37/4 No. 37415 crosses the causeway at Fernaig (8 miles from Kyle) with the 17.00 Kyle to Dingwall train. This location is inside the grounds of the Highland Farm animal sanctuary. Note that the train is made up of green and cream liveried excursion coaching stock, specially for use on the Kyle route.

Our second photograph on the Kyle line was taken at Garve. Like the photograph above, it shows the rugged Highland scenery on this attractive line. The train is once again the 17.00 Kyle to Dingwall service (complete with excursion stock), and is seen pulling out of Garve station on the evening of 1 August 1989. In charge is English Electric Class 37/4 No. 37417 *Highland Region*. At the time the Kyle trains (and those from Wick and Thurso) terminated at Dingwall owing to the collapse of the bridge over the River Ness at Inverness the previous February. A replacement bridge was opened the following year. Worthy of note is the Highland Railway footbridge.

Throughout most of the 1980s the line to Oban from Glasgow and Crianlarich had locomotive-hauled trains, and on 28 July 1988, in typical Highland scenery (and weather), we see Class 37/4 No. 37424 *Glendarroch* on the Oban branch between Dalmally and Tyndrum with the 08.10 Oban to Glasgow train. Note the West Highland Terrier emblem on the side of the locomotive.

During the 1980s there was still some freight working on the Oban branch. On 27 July 1988, Class 37/4 No. 37410 *Aluminium 100* is seen leaving Crianlarich (lower yard) and just about to join the Oban line with an afternoon tank train for Oban. In the background is the metal viaduct which carries the Crianlarich to Fort William line. Crianlarich lower yard is the last remaining section of the old Caledonian line from Callander and Dunblane which, because of landslips, closed in 1965.

English Electric Type 4 Class 50 locomotive No. 50014 *Warspite* heads down the grade towards the site of Brent station with the (Fridays only) 17.55 Plymouth to Paddington train on 5 April 1985. In the background is the edge of Dartmoor National Park. Brent was once the junction for the branch line to Kingsbridge. The branch closed in 1963, and Brent station closed the following year.

   The Class 50s were first introduced in 1967. Of the fifty members of the class, the first three were withdrawn from service in 1987, including No. 50014 in December of that year.

On the evening of 8 April 1985 Class 50 No. 50047 *Swiftsure* with the 13.40 Paddington to Penzance service threads its way along the Teign estuary at Bishopsteignton, between Teignmouth and Newton Abbot.

The last Saturday of the BR winter timetable, 14 May 1988, saw the virtual end of the Class 33 workings on the Cardiff to Portsmouth trains. On that day No. 33211 is seen in an attractive setting at Claverton (south-east of Bath) with the 16.20 Cardiff to Portsmouth service. In the foreground is the Kennet & Avon Canal, and just above the train can be seen the River Avon, both waterways running in parallel for several miles along this lovely West Country valley.

One of the early Type 3 English Electric Class 37 locomotives, No. 37021, and Class 47 No. 47205 are caught by the camera as they leave Slochd Viaduct and head down towards Aviemore with the 14.30 Inverness to Perth train. This location is just south of Slochd summit, which has an elevation of 1,315ft. The snow is still on the hillsides in this early springtime photograph, taken on 4 April 1986. Like their more powerful brothers, the English Electric Class 40s, the Class 37s show several front-end design variations.

A busy scene at Crianlarich station on 27 July 1988. Class 37/4 No. 37422 waits to head south to Glasgow with a tank train from Oban as Class 37/4 No. 37401 *Mary Queen of Scots* approaches the station with the 10.04 Glasgow (Queen Street) to Fort William train, a journey of 122 miles, with arrival in Fort William at 13.57.

The evening sunshine highlights the 18.10 Thurso to Georgemas Junction train as it approaches the junction on 3 April 1989 hauled by Class 37/4 No. 37415. At the junction, No. 37415 will reverse the train onto the rear of the 18.00 service from Wick (hauled by Class 37/4 No. 37421) to form the 18.27 to Dingwall with No. 37421 in charge. (See lower photograph on page 136.)

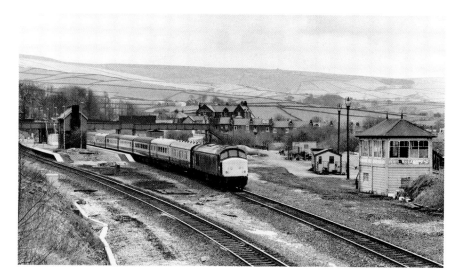

Chinley, in north-west Derbyshire, is situated on the Manchester to Sheffield (Hope Valley) route, which runs through the Peak District. It is also the junction for the freight-only line to Dove Holes and Buxton. On 1 April 1983 Peak Class 45/1 No. 45120 hurries through the remains of Chinley station with the 09.32 Nottingham to Glasgow service. This train ran via Sheffield, Manchester, Preston and then the WCML to Glasgow.

Another route from the Manchester area to Yorkshire is the Diggle or Standedge line. This route carries a lot of the traffic from the north-east of England to Manchester and Liverpool. The lower slopes of the Pennine hills form a backdrop as an unidentified Class 45 approaches Standedge Tunnel at Marsden with a morning Scarborough to Liverpool train on 5 March 1983. The tunnel itself is 3 miles 66yd long and, as can be seen, there were once four tracks through the (then) three tunnels. Only the double-track tunnel is in use; the other two closed in October 1966. The former warehouse on the Huddersfield & Ashton Canal on the left is now a visitor centre and is at the start of the longest and deepest canal tunnel in Britain, running from Marsden to Diggle.

Winter and spring weather are illustrated in these two scenes, photographed between Banbury and Birmingham on the former GWR route to Paddington. The top photograph shows Class 50 No. 50034 *Furious* as it climbs the 1 in 110 of Hatton Bank (north-west of Warwick) heading for Tyseley with the ECS of a Paddington to Leamington Spa special Pullman train on 16 February 1983. Class 50s saw regular work on this route throughout the 1980s. This line is also used by cross-country trains from the north to the south of England. The view above, taken on 27 May 1989, shows Class 47 No. 47652 as it heads south through Harbury cutting (north of Banbury) with the 07.48 York to Poole service.

The rugged country west of Arisaig on the Fort William to Mallaig line provides the backdrop as Class 37/4 No. 37423 *Sir Murray Morrison 1874–1948*, in grey freight livery, heads for Mallaig with the 16.10 train from Fort William on 13 August 1988.

The sun is setting over the Isle of Skye as Class 37/4 No. 37417 *Highland Region* runs towards Kyle of Lochalsh with the 18.22 train from Dingwall on 31 July 1989. The location is Badicaul, just to the east of the Kyle.

Chapter Three
Deltics

The station clock says five past two as English Electric Type 5 Deltic Class No. 55016 *Gordon Highlander* pulls out of Kings Cross station with the 14.05 train to York on Saturday 20 June 1981. On the right-hand side is Brush Type 2 No. 31408 on an ECS train. This would be the last summer that the mighty Deltic locomotives would work out of Kings Cross, being withdrawn from service by the following January. The Deltics were first introduced in 1961 to replace the former LNER Pacific steam locomotives on the East Coast Main Line (ECML) between London and Scotland. In all, twenty-two members of the class were built.

The scenes on this page and opposite were taken on Saturday 20 June 1981 at Kings Cross station. *Left:* the contrasting front ends of Class 55 No. 55016 and Class 31 No. 31408 as they pause after arriving with morning trains from York and the east of England respectively.

Below: a midday train arrives from York with Deltic No. 55009 *Alycidon* in charge. On the left is a Class 47 locomotive.

Half an hour later *(opposite top)* No. 55009 has been joined by No. 55015 *Tulyar* on an arrival from the north-east. Note the plaque on the front of No. 55015 to denote that the locomotive took part in the cavalcade at Rainhill in 1980 to celebrate the 150th anniversary of the Liverpool & Manchester Railway, 'Rocket 150'.

Opposite below: Deltic locomotive No. 55015.

Kings Cross has never been the same without the roar of the Deltic locomotives' twin Napier engines as they departed for the north-east and Scotland.

This photograph of Deltic No. 55014 *The Duke of Wellington's Regiment* pulling out of Selby on the afternoon of 23 May 1981 with a Kings Cross to York train gives a good idea of the size of these huge locomotives. It is about to cross over Selby swing bridge and under the overhead signal-box. *Opposite top:* The same train with No. 55014 entering Selby station.

Opposite below: The next day, 24 May, sees No. 55016 *Gordon Highlander* entering Selby station with the 11.43 York to Kings Cross train. Note the two signal-boxes, the attractive station awnings and the railway official on the right wearing the BR uniform of the day.

In 1983 this section of the ECML from Selby to Chaloners Whin Junction was closed and a new line constructed to the west of Selby from Colton Junction (5 miles south of York) to Doncaster via Temple Hirst Junction (on the ECML north of Doncaster), thus avoiding the bottleneck at Selby where the busy Leeds to Hull line also runs through.

One of the finest sights of the 1980s was to see a southbound Deltic-hauled train departing from York. On the evening of 24 May 1981, No. 55007 *Pinza* makes a splendid sight (and sound) as it pulls out of the city's imposing station with the 19.10 train to Kings Cross. Overlooking the scene is the beautiful medieval York Minster.

Our old friend No. 55007 again, this time on 26 August 1981 as it shunts empty coaching stock across the bridge over the River Ouse at the northern end of York station on the Scarborough line.

In the last few months of their active life the Deltic locomotives ran many special trains to all parts of the BR system. On 24 October 1981 No. 55015 *Tulyar* is seen at one of York's outer platforms, waiting to leave with a special charter train to Aberdeen, 'The Deltic Salute', organised by the Deltic Preservation Society. Happily, several members of the class have been preserved and examples can be seen from time to time on main-line charter trains.

Chapter Four
Viaducts & Bridges

The Royal Border Bridge, just south of the ancient Border town of Berwick-upon-Tweed, is the setting as an HST unit heads south on 28 May 1987 with the 06.50 Aberdeen to Kings Cross train. With an arrival in the capital at 14.25, just over 7½ hours is allowed for the 524-mile journey.

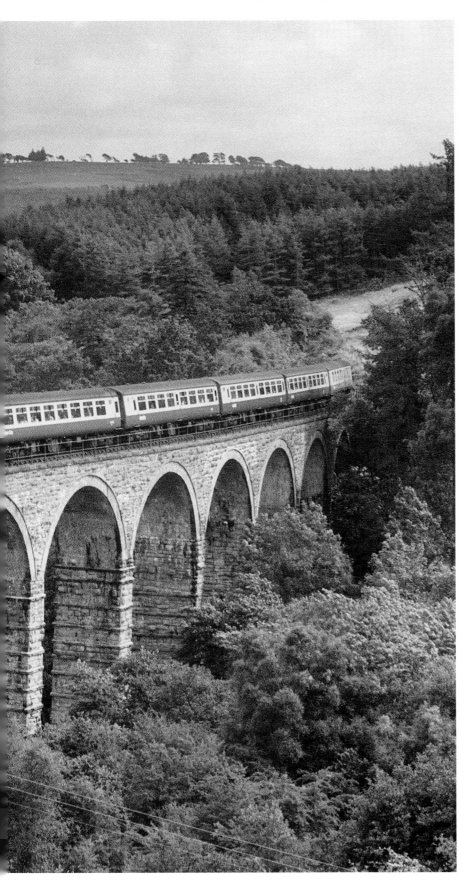

Class 47/4 No. 47457 crosses the attractive viaduct at Pinmore with the 14.25 Stranraer to Glasgow service on 29 July 1987. The viaduct is situated between Barrhill and Girvan on the former Glasgow & South Western Railway (G&SWR) line, which connects Glasgow with the port of Stranraer for the ferry services to Larne in Northern Ireland. This viaduct, one of several on this picturesque route, is regarded as one of the most graceful and photogenic in Scotland.

Another impressive stone viaduct, this time at Chester-le-Street, just north of Durham on the ECML. A Metropolitan-Cammell Class 101 unit, with car No. 54219 leading, crosses over this fine structure on the evening of 11 August 1986 with the 17.25 Newcastle to Durham service. Chester-le-Street is also the home of Durham County Cricket Club, the picturesque test match ground being called The Riverside.

The S&C line between Settle Junction and Carlisle has a great many viaducts of all sizes. The small but attractive viaduct of Eden Lacey, south of Lazonby, crosses the River Eden; it is 137yd long and 60ft high. Seen running over the viaduct on 6 May 1989 is Class 47 No. 47818 with a twelve-coach special charter train, 'The Settle–Carlisle Express', from the south of England to Carlisle, organised by Victoria Travel. Note that the locomotive is turned out in InterCity livery.

At 7.35 p.m. on Saturday 1 August 1987 Class 45/1 No. 45104 *Royal Warwickshire Fusiliers* is caught by the evening sun as it crosses Durham Viaduct. It is about to enter Durham station with the 09.25 (Saturdays Only) Newquay to Newcastle train. Timetabled locomotive-hauled trains to Newquay ceased at the end of the 1987 summer timetable, when run-round facilities were withdrawn from Newquay station.

The Type 4 Class 45s were built by BR at its Crewe and Derby works between 1960 and 1962, and the name 'Peak' came into being because the first eight locomotives were named after mountains in the Peak District.

The Cornish main line has even more viaducts than the S&C route, and among its finest must be Lynher Viaduct, 4 miles west of Saltash. The late afternoon spring sunshine highlights the 14.55 St Blazey to Gloucester goods, hauled by Class 37/5s No. 37672 *Freight Transport Association* and No. 37674 as they head off Lynher Viaduct on 13 April 1988. This eight-arch viaduct crosses the River Lynher, which has its source on Bodmin Moor and joins the River Tamar at Saltash.

This photograph, taken from Crianlarich lower goods yard, shows the 08.40 Fort William to Glasgow train as it crosses the metal viaduct just to the north of Crianlarich station on 27 July 1988. It is hauled by Class 37/4 No. 37423 *Sir Murray Morrison*.

These English Electric Type 3 locomotives were first introduced in 1957, and a few members of the class can still be seen today on Britain's railways. Many examples have survived into preservation. The class is also known by three nicknames – 'Growlers', 'Syphons' and 'Tractors'.

One of the world's most famous bridges – the Forth Bridge – dwarfs Class 27 locomotive No. 27018 as it approaches North Queensferry station with a midday Edinburgh to Dundee train on 11 May 1983. These Type 2 locomotives were built by Birmingham RC&W in 1961, and were a development of the earlier Class 26 locomotives. They had been withdrawn by the late 1980s. Four examples remain in preservation.

On 29 August 1986 'Growler' No. 37414 crosses the Kyle of Sutherland at Invershin with the 11.35 Inverness to Wick and Thurso train. At both ends of this bridge there are stations, Invershin to the north and Culrain to the south, and they are around half a mile apart. Note the ScotRail emblem on the side of the rear cab. From the summer of 1989 passenger traffic on the Far North route was in the hands of Sprinter units.

The locks at Banavie, just west of Fort William on the Mallaig line, are the setting as a southbound goods from Corpach, hauled by Class 37/4 No. 37412 *Loch Lomond*, crosses the swingbridge on 4 June 1986. This flight of locks is known as Neptune's Staircase, and connects the Caledonian Canal in the foreground to Loch Linnhe, a sea loch.

Class 37/5 No. 37675 shunts tented clay wagons on the Moorswater branch line near ECC Moorswater driers on 27 August 1988. These tented wagons were replaced a few weeks after this photograph was taken. Overlooking the scene is the graceful Moorswater Viaduct, which is situated to the west of Liskeard station on the Cornish main line to Penzance. Note the piers of the original Brunel-built timber viaduct.

On 11 May 1983 Birmingham RC&W Type 2 Class 26 No. 26008 crosses over the 550-ft long Jameson Viaduct on the climb out of Inverkeithing and heads for North Queensferry and the Forth Bridge with a neat-looking southbound track train. These locomotives were first introduced in 1958/59 and remained in service until the early 1990s. Several examples of the class have been preserved.

One of the earlier examples of the English Electric Class 37s, No. 37047, heads over the High Level Bridge across the River Tyne on 11 August 1986 and approaches Newcastle Central station with a rail maintenance train. This photograph, which was taken from the castle keep, would today, with the electrification of the ECML in the late 1980s, show much catenary and wires.

The background architecture is also of interest, with a mixture of Victorian buildings and 1960s high-rise flats. At the far end of the bridge the junction for the Sunderland line (left) and the ECML (right) can be seen.

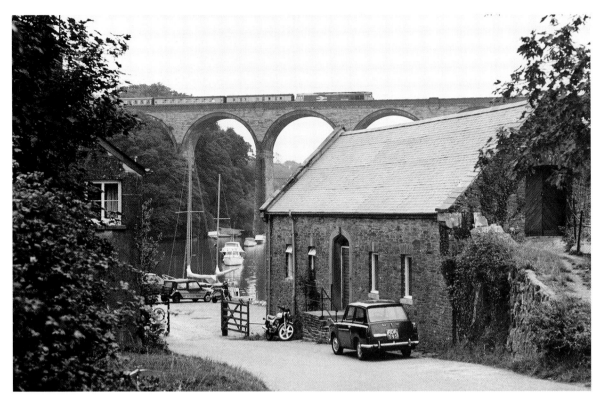

The photographs on this page were taken on 9 August 1984 at St Germans Viaduct, around 5 miles west of Saltash on the Plymouth to Penzance route. The scene *(above)* shows English Electric Class 50 No. 50008 *Thunderer* as it crosses the viaduct with the 16.15 Penzance to Paddington train. In the foreground, an Austin A40 car gives the view a 1960s feel.

A few minutes earlier, and we see an unidentified Class 45 (believed to be No. 45004 *Royal Irish Fusilier*) crossing the viaduct from the Saltash side *(below)* with the 12.02 Birmingham New Street to Penzance train. In this photograph, a variety of boats provides the foreground interest.

Another fine selection of boats, this time at Hayle harbour on 30 May 1985. Crossing over the 227-yd long Hayle Viaduct is Class 50 No. 50006 *Neptune* with the 16.35 Plymouth to Penzance service. In a few minutes the train will be arriving at the Cornish terminus at the scheduled time of 18.59.

An immaculate Class 37/4 No. 37429 *Eisteddfod Genedlaethol* crosses the Usk river bridge at Newport with the 10.45 Cardiff to Crewe service on 25 September 1987. This attractive journey threads the ancient border area between Wales and England. The Class 37s took over these Welsh Marches trains in the early/mid-1980s from the Class 33s, only to be superseded in the early 1990s by Sprinter units.

On 1 April 1983 Class 47/4 No. 47436 crosses over Saddleworth Viaduct on the Manchester to Huddersfield line (via Stalybridge) with an afternoon Liverpool to Newcastle train. Below the viaduct is the Huddersfield & Ashton Canal. The Class 47s were built by Brush Traction, Loughborough, or at BR Crewe Works, between 1963 and 1967, and some members of this once-extensive class can still be seen today at work on Britain's railways.

The final view in this chapter shows once again the massive Royal Border Bridge at Berwick, only this time from the western side. Crossing the bridge in the evening sunshine on 31 July 1987 is the 18.47 Berwick to Newcastle local train, hauled by Class 47/4 No. 47661.

Chapter Five

Signal-boxes & Semaphore Signals

One of the major changes that occurred on BR in the 1980s was the signalling modernisation plan. This affected many areas, including the East Midlands, East Anglia, some parts of Wales and northern Scotland, but perhaps had the greatest impact on the former GWR West of England main line from Westbury through to Totnes, the short section from Totnes to Plymouth having already been modernised.

One of the principal locations covered by the modernisation plan was the Newton Abbot area, which up until 1987 had a wonderful selection of semaphore signals and boxes. Framed by part of the former GWR signal gantry at the eastern end of Newton Abbot, Class 47/4 No. 47627 *City of Oxford* runs smoothly into Newton Abbot station on Saturday 31 August 1985 with the 12.02 Birmingham New Street to Penzance train. Note the GWR signal-box, to the left of which (out of sight) is the freight-only line to Heathfield. This line was part of the Teign Valley line to Exeter and also the branch line to Moreton-hampstead, which ran from Heathfield, but both these lines had closed by 1964.

On 23 July 1989 the 20.25 sleeper train from Fort William to Euston approaches Mallaig Junction on the outskirts of Fort William, hauled by Class 37/4 No. 37413 *Loch Eil Outward Bound*. On the left is a BR semaphore signal with a North British lattice post. This sleeper train and the one from Paddington to Penzance still run today, but at the time of writing there is much talk of discontinuing this fine service.

The North British signal-box at Banavie, just to the west of Fort William, is the location as Class 37/4 No. 37422 crosses Banavie swingbridge with the 10.05 Fort William to Mallaig train on 28 August 1986.

The Highland main line from Perth still had several locomotive-hauled trains throughout the 1980s and also, in certain locations, signal-boxes and semaphore signals. One such place was the station area at the small village of Dalwhinnie, which is situated just off the main A9 trunk road from Perth to Inverness. On 2 August 1989 Class 47/4 No. 47541 *The Queen Mother (above)* is about to pass the signal-box and enter Dalwhinnie station with the 14.45 Inverness to Edinburgh train.

Although the former Midland Railway (MR) signal-box *(below)* at Dent station on the S&C closed in 1980, it remained in situ for several years before it was finally demolished by burning. On 27 July 1983 Peak Class 45/1 No. 45115 powers its way past Dent box with the 16.00 Leeds to Carlisle train. The box, although not having been in use for some three years, still seems to be in reasonable order.

I well remember visiting this location on 15 September 1966, when the friendly signalman invited me in for a look around and a chat, and later I took a photograph from the steps of the signal-box of Jubilee Class 4–6–0 No. 45675 *Hardy* climbing up to Dent with the 09.15 Leeds to Carlisle parcels train.

This was taken from inside the London Brighton South Coast Railway (LBSCR) signal-box at Birchden Junction (by kind permission of BR). Approaching the box is Class 207 East Sussex three-car unit No. 1319, forming the 14.34 Eridge to Tunbridge Wells West service on 31 August 1983. These units were built in 1962 at BR Eastleigh Works. Birchden was also the junction for the line to Oxted (from Uckfield), but the line to Tunbridge Wells was closed some years ago and then reopened as a preserved line, the Spa Valley Railway, with trains running from Groombridge (to the east of Birchden Junction) to Tunbridge Wells West.

The line from Oxted to Uckfield originally ran to Lewes, but this section closed in the 1960s, leaving Uckfield as the terminus for trains to London. On the evening of 31 August 1983 Class 33 No. 33058 is about to pass the LBSCR signal-box as it pulls out of Uckfield with the 19.10 train to East Croydon, having earlier worked in with the 17.20 train from London Bridge. Note the crossing gates, which at the time were still operated by a wheel in the signal-box. On the left is Class 205 Hampshire three-car unit No. 1120 (built at Eastleigh in 1957), which had just arrived with the 17.36 from London Bridge.

During the summer of 1983, there were just eight Class 33 weekday turns on passenger trains between London Bridge/East Croydon and the East Grinstead and Uckfield lines, the rest of the commuter trains being in the hands of DMUs. The Type 3 Class 33 locomotives were built by Birmingham RC&W between 1960 and 1962, and are popularly known as 'Cromptons' because of their Crompton–Parkinson electrical equipment.

Framed by typical Southern Railway (SR) rail-built bracket signals, Class 73 electro-diesel No. 73126 pulls away from Redhill station and heads northwards on 1 September 1983. Note the SR disc signals, and also the pre-war SR signal-box.

The Class 73 locomotives were built by English Electric during 1962 to 1966 and some can still be seen at work on Britain's railways today. For many years they ran on the 'Gatwick Express' trains from Victoria to Gatwick Airport.

Class 47 No. 47222 heads though Barnetby at 4 p.m. on the afternoon of 26 July 1983 with an eastbound tank train. At the rear of the train can be seen the cluster of semaphore signals which control Wrawby Junction, the junction for the lines to Doncaster, Gainsborough and Lincoln respectively, all former Great Central routes.

The cathedral city of Ely in the heart of the Fens was well known among railway enthusiasts for its splendid Great Eastern signal-boxes, and also its quantity of semaphore signals, which survived until electrification of the route from Liverpool Street to King's Lynn in the early 1990s. On the evening of 22 July 1983 Class 47 No. 47085 *Mammoth* approaches Ely South box and is about to enter Ely station with the 18.35 London Liverpool Street to Ely train. Note the silver roof of the locomotive, a characteristic of Stratford's Class 47 fleet. Completing the scene is a variety of former London North Eastern Railway (LNER) semaphore signals.

On 17 April 1984 Class 47 No. 47291 and brake van head through Bedale on their journey from Tees yard to Redmire. This branch, which leaves the ECML just north of Northallerton, was once part of the North Eastern line to Hawes and on to Garsdale on the S&C route. In the foreground is an LNER wooden post bracket signal, beyond which are two North Eastern signals with lattice posts, and on the right is a more modern LNER semaphore signal. The 16-mile section from Leeming Bar (6 miles west of Northallerton) to Redmire is now privately leased and known as the Wensleydale Railway plc with several examples of DMUs and diesel locomotives preserved and working there. This railway has also leased the section between Leeming Bar and Castle Hills, Northallerton.

The photographs opposite and above were taken near Carnforth on the Furness line on 29 September 1983. The first scene *(opposite)* shows Class 47 No. 47077 passing under a fine example of an ex-LMS left-hand bracket signal with an afternoon mixed freight train for the shipbuilding town of Barrow-in-Furness. A few minutes later Type 2 Class 25/2 No. 25161 *(above)* heads for Barrow with a ballast train.

The Class 25s, or 'Rats' as they were popularly known, were first introduced in 1961 and were withdrawn by the mid-1980s. They were built by BR at their Crewe, Darlington and Derby works, and were a development of the earlier Class 24 design. Several examples remain in preservation.

Although the semaphore signals at Stourbridge Junction on the former GWR Birmingham to Kidderminster/ Worcester line disappeared in the 1970s, the signal-box remained and is still there today. On a bright day, 18 January 1984, Class 25/2 No. 25244 heads towards the goods yard, which is situated beyond the signal-box. On the right is Brush Type 2 Class 31 No. 31126 with a goods train for Wolverhampton. On entering the station No. 31126 will run round its train and then head north for Wolverhampton via Dudley and Bescot (Walsall). This station is also the junction for Stourbridge Town, the short branch line (out of sight) running to the left of the GWR signal-box. This is worked by a single-car unit.

Another fine GWR signal-box, this time at the eastern end of Truro station. On Wednesday 30 May 1984 Class 45/1 No. 45139 approaches Truro station with the 09.21 Leeds to Penzance train. Just to the right of the locomotive can be seen Truro Cathedral. Note also, on the left, the freight line, which has now been taken up.

Sadly the semaphore signals in the Exeter area had, with the signalling modernisation scheme, disappeared by the middle of 1985. However, when this photograph was taken on Saturday 26 May 1984, they were all more or less still intact, including this beautiful GWR bracket signal situated at the north end of Exeter St Davids station. Passing this 'Christmas tree' of a signal is Class 50 No. 50015 *Valiant* with the 08.55 Paignton to Paddington train.

The fourth photograph in this quartet of GWR boxes and signals was taken at Worcester Shrub Hill station on 17 June 1983, and shows Class 25/2 No. 25097 with a southbound midday parcels train. Happily, the fine array of signals is still there today, as are the two signal-boxes (out of sight) which control the same.

We leave the former GWR lines and head to the north-east of England, first to Haltwhistle on the former North Eastern Carlisle to Newcastle line. In the station on 15 August 1983 a Class 101 two-car DMU is about to depart with the 14.43 Carlisle to Newcastle service. Overlooking the scene is a fine example of a North Eastern signal-box. Note also the staggered platform layout and the splendid footbridge. At one time Haltwhistle was the junction station for the branch line to Alston (to the south), which closed in 1976, but the trackbed of this branch between Alston and Kirkhaugh now plays host to a fine miniature railway, the South Tynedale Railway.

The photographs left and opposite, taken on 8 August 1986, show the continental-style LNER signal-box at Northallerton on the ECML in North Yorkshire. The first scene *(left)*, shows Class 45/1 No. 45124 as it departs from the station with the 11.12 Bangor to Newcastle train.

A few minutes earlier sees Class 31 No. 31277 *(opposite)* with a short southbound freight train, framed by the new and old as it crosses the junction for Stockton (to the north-east) and approaches Northallerton station.

English Electric Class 50 No. 50016 *Barham* is framed by a former GWR bracket signal (now with upper quadrant semaphore blades, owing to regional changes) as it approaches Aynho Junction with the 10.09 Birmingham New Street to Paddington train on 21 January 1984. Note the GWR lower quadrant signal to the left of the locomotive.

Class 47 No. 47225 passes the new power box at Westbury as it approaches the station with an empty stone train from the Paddington direction on 26 May 1983. The line on the left is to Bath Spa and Bristol. Within a few months the new signal-box would be in use and the semaphore signals would all disappear from the area, quickly making this an historic scene.

This LNER 'gallows' signal dominates the foreground as English Electric Class 08 No. 08407 pauses during shunting duties in Ipswich yard (near East Suffolk Junction) on 5 August 1983.

The Class 08 shunters were built between 1952 and 1962 and although many of this once-numerous class have been withdrawn, there are still some at work today on Britain's railways. Several are also in private industrial use and some members of the class have been preserved.

Class 45 No. 45022 *Lytham St Anne's* gives off a fair amount of exhaust as it pulls out of Taunton on 11 April 1983 with a Newcastle to Plymouth train. This signal gantry is a fine example of post-1922 GWR signalling. With resignalling in the area in the mid-1980s, scenes like this were soon to become a memory.

A newly built Class 58 No. 58002 was a surprise visitor to the south-west of England on 1 September 1984. The location is Aller Junction, near Newton Abbot, and the train is the 12.10 Liverpool Lime Street to Plymouth HST service which had failed at Birmingham New Street station and was being towed from there to Plymouth by this 3,300hp freight locomotive.

The powerful Class 58 locomotives were built by British Rail Engineering Ltd (BREL) at its Doncaster works between 1983 and 1987. There were fifty locomotives in this class and they survived until about 2003, their replacements being the Canadian-built Class 66 locomotives, which were introduced in the late 1990s. The semaphore signals at Aller and the surrounding area survived until April 1987.

The splendid semaphore signals at Inverness survived until the end of 1986, including this fine gantry signal adjacent to Welshs Bridge signal-box, just to the east of Inverness station. The signal-box is of Highland Railway design, and the gantry has a good array of lattice post-supported home, distant and calling-on signals. To complete the scene, Class 47/4 No. 47441 is seen on 20 August 1983 heading east towards the diesel depot, which is behind the photographer. Note also the gantry signal in the distance and the bracket signal at the other side of the box.

On 11 July 1984 Class 47/3 No. 47364 approaches Bolton station from the Manchester area with a short north-bound midday tank train. Overlooking the scene is a handsome ex-LMS gantry signal.

The ex-LNWR signal-boxes in and around Chester General station, in particular the high Chester No. 2 and Chester No. 6 boxes, situated at opposite ends of the station, are shown in the photographs on these two pages. *Opposite:* this scene (taken with a telephoto lens) shows a tight fit as Class 47/4 No. 47445 edges its way around No. 2 box as it pulls out of Chester on 22 October 1983 with the 14.25 Holyhead to Crewe train. *Above:* another view of No. 2 box, this time on 6 July 1983 as Class 47/4 No. 47512 pulls out of Chester General station with the 09.15 Bangor to Manchester Victoria train. On the right is the station goods yard, where a Class 25 is seen shunting parcels vans.

The final photograph in this trio shows Class 47 No. 47266 heading west out of Chester and passing Chester No. 6 box with a coal train bound for the North Wales area on the evening of 13 July 1983.

This chapter ends with a view of a BR Swindon-built Class 124 four-car Trans-Pennine unit as it passes under the North Eastern signal-box at Selby swingbridge with an afternoon York to Liverpool train on 5 March 1983. These units were first introduced in 1959.

Chapter Six
Freight Trains

We start this section on freight trains with an old-and-new view. This lovely old GWR footbridge at Albrighton station, on the Wolverhampton to Shrewsbury line, frames at the time one of BR's latest fleet of freight locomotives – the Class 58s. No. 58043 heads south at Albrighton on 1 July 1987 with a merry-go-round (MGR) empty coal train from Ironbridge power station. The junction for Ironbridge power station is Madeley Junction, just to the north-west of Shifnal. This line originally ran down to Much Wenlock and on to Craven Arms, but these lines had closed by 1962.

Our next location is Standish Junction, south of Gloucester, where the Swindon and Bristol lines part company. On the evening of 20 August 1985 Peak Class No. 45142 approaches the junction from the Swindon direction with a Swindon to Longbridge (for British Leyland) Speedlink Railfreight service. With the closure of the Rover factory at Longbridge, these freight workings will now be a thing of the past.

Opposite: A not uncommon sight in the West Country in the 1980s was a powerful locomotive with a tiny load. Type 4 Class 50 No. 50015 *Valiant* is caught by the camera as it heads for Plymouth on 6 May 1988. The location is Coldrenick (just east of Liskeard) and the train is the 13.15 Penzance to Bristol van(s) train. A very light load for 2,700hp, but on some days this train would be loaded with up to twelve vehicles. At the rear of the picture can be seen Tresulgan Viaduct.

On 5 August 1983, Class 31 No. 31184 leaves Ipswich Tunnel and approaches Ipswich station with a Down evening van train.

The Type 2 Class 31 locomotives were built by Brush Traction, Loughborough, between 1957 and 1962, and a few members of the class can still be seen at work today on the main line. Like many classes of diesel locomotives, several examples have been preserved.

A nicely turned-out pair of Class 37 locomotives, No. 37083 (in blue livery) and No. 37202 (in grey freight livery), is seen in charge of a Scunthorpe to Cardiff steel train on 30 May 1989. The train is just south of Bromsgrove at Stoke Prior on the former MR Birmingham to Bristol main line.

The reader will no doubt have noticed that some of the Class 37s and also some of the other classes have an extra number after the Type, e.g. Class 37/4; this generally denotes a refurbishment on the locomotive.

On Sunday 21 June 1987 Class 37 No. 37117 heads along the ECML to the north of Berwick-upon-Tweed, near Lamberton on the Scottish border, with a northbound coal train. Within a few weeks of this photograph being taken this section of the line was electrified as part of the ECML electrification scheme.

An interesting train, which could be classified as a freight working, was the Motorail which from 1982 ran from Paddington to St Austell with passengers travelling separately by normal HST service. Before 1982 the train operated from Kensington in London with provision for passengers to travel on carriages attached to the train.

The first scene *(above)* shows the return Motorail car carrier service from St Austell to Paddington as it descends Rattery Bank near Totnes on Saturday 18 August 1984 with Class 47/4 No. 47513 *Severn* in charge. On 11 August 1984 *(below)* Class 37 No. 37096 sets off from the Down platform at St Austell to enter the Motorail sidings (to the right of the Up platform) with the Paddington to St Austell Motorail train. At the rear of the photograph on the right is the space once occupied by the original Motorail sidings, for use by the Motorail passenger carriages and car transporter wagons. Note the GWR footbridge, station buildings and canopies.

It was quite rare to see a
Class 56 freight locomotive
in the south-west, because
other than a few examples
based at Cardiff Canton
depot, most of the 135
members of this class,
certainly during the late
1980s, were shedded at
Toton depot in the east
Midlands. However, while
photographing around
Totnes on 31 December
1987 I was lucky to see one
of Cardiff's Class 56s,
No. 56050, as it left Totnes
station and started to
climb Rattery Bank with
a Plymouth-bound
freight train.

The late-evening sun highlights Class 56 No. 56130 as it leaves the Manchester to Chester/North Wales main
line at Helsby Junction on 13 October 1989 and heads for Ellesmere Port with loaded coal wagons.

   The Class 56 locomotives were built between 1976 and 1984, either in Romania (as sub-contractors for Brush)
or by BREL at its Crewe or Doncaster works and, owing to their radiator and front-end airhorn grilles, are
nicknamed 'Grids' or 'Gridirons'.

The two views on this page were photographed at Fairwood Junction, to the west of Westbury, on 16 June 1989.

The scene here shows Class 56 No. 56053 *Sir Morgannwg Ganol/County of Mid Glamorgan* leaving the Westbury area with an evening Down empty stone train, probably bound for the Amey Roadstone Corporation (ARC) quarry at Whatley, to the west of Frome. On the right is the Westbury avoiding line, part of the former GWR West of England main line to Plymouth and Penzance. Note in the background the Westbury White Horse carved into the hillside.

The view from the opposite direction shows Class 56 No. 56045 as it takes the line to Westbury station at Fairwood Junction with an Up morning stone train from Foster Yeoman's quarry at Merehead (south of Frome, near Cranmore) to Acton freightyard.

Like the Deltics and Class 58 locomotives, these powerful locomotives are classified as Type 5. Most, if not all, of the class have now been withdrawn, but several examples have been preserved, including No. 56045.

Nechells power station and the M6 motorway provide an imposing industrial background as an unidentified Peak Class 45 locomotive shunts a coal train in Washwood Heath sidings at Bromford Bridge in east Birmingham, on the line to Derby and Leicester on 14 April 1982.

A train of ECC 'Tiger' tanks from St Blazey yard to Stoke-on-Trent hurries past the harbour at Cockwood, just west of Starcross, during the evening of 12 April 1983. In charge is a Peak Class locomotive.

Another freight by the sea, this time on the sea wall to the east of Dawlish station. Class 47 No. 47145 heads for Exeter Riverside goods yard with a mixed midday goods train from Plymouth on a sunny 12 February 1988.

Class 47s, like most of the diesels, have a nickname. They are known as 'Duffs', a term which I well remember being used by steam fans when the 47s began replacing steam locomotives in the early to mid-1960s.

Redhill on the London (Victoria) to Brighton main line is also the junction station for Guildford to the west and Tonbridge to the east. This view, looking north, was taken at Redhill station on 1 September 1983 and shows Class 33 No. 33050 waiting to leave with a southbound tank train. Note the station architecture dating back to pre-grouping days.

In the 1980s the Aberdeen to Inverness route saw a reasonable amount of freight workings, including wood trains. This busy scene to the east of Inverurie station, on 3 April 1986, shows English Electric Class 20 locomotives Nos 20114 and 20123 waiting for the 11.40 Aberdeen to Inverness train, hauled by Class 47 No. 47049, to clear the single-line section and enter Inverurie station, before they can leave with a wood train from the Elgin area to Aberdeen. The Class 20s were built between 1957 and 1967, and because of their engine sound are known as 'Choppers'.

Class 25/3 No. 25324 approaches Chester from the west with a trip working from Llandudno Junction on the evening of 13 July 1983. The train has just crossed over the 'Roodee' (see top picture on page 13) and shortly will be crossing over the Shropshire Union Canal at Northgate lock, before threading through the walls of this Roman city and entering Chester General station.

The Droitwich radio masts overlook the Bristol to Birmingham main line at Stoke Prior, south of Bromsgrove, as Class 47 No. 47222 *Appleby-Frodingham* heads towards Birmingham on 30 May 1989 with a South Wales to Immingham freight train.

Class 40 No. 40001 brightens up a very wet and gloomy day as it passes through Plumpton Junction on 19 April 1984 with a goods train from Barrow to Carnforth. Plumpton Junction is situated just to the east of Ulverston, and was the junction for the line to Haverthwaite and Windermere Lakeside. After closure of this line in the 1960s Windermere Lakeside to Haverthwaite was preserved, and is now known as the Lakeside & Haverthwaite Railway. The line running off to the left of the picture is the short branch to the Glaxo works.

The storm clouds are gathering over the hills of the Derbyshire Peak District as Class 25/2 No. 25161 runs through the remains of Chinley station on 1 April 1983 with a mineral train from Peak Forest to the Manchester area. As can be seen, this once busy junction station originally had four tracks running through it, but with rationalisation two of these were removed in about 1980.

This photograph was taken at the western end of Manchester Victoria station on 27 June 1984, and shows Class 40 No. 40035 with an eastbound empty stone train bound for Chinley and Peak Forest via Miles Platting, Ashburys, Marple and New Mills.

During the early 1980s it was often possible to see Class 25s at work on the Settle & Carlisle route. On the morning of 5 November 1983 Class 25/2 No. 25185 heads away from Blea Moor sidings and approaches Ribblehead (or Batty Moss) Viaduct with a ballast train from Ribblehead quarry. The quarry is south of the viaduct, but the train will have travelled the short distance north over Ribblehead Viaduct to Blea Moor sidings to gain the Up, or southbound, line.

Class 56 No. 56069 runs by the side of the old signal-box at Water Orton on 6 May 1987 with an empty coal train bound for the Leicester area. At the time this BR-style signal-box was used as a tool store, and lasted many years in this capacity until it was finally demolished in the summer of 1999. Note (at the rear) the handsome station entrance and ticket office of Midland Railway design.

Class 58 No. 58032 powers its way up Hatton Bank on the former GWR Banbury to Birmingham Snow Hill main line with a northbound MGR train on 13 May 1989. These Type 5 locomotives are nicknamed 'Fitted Wardrobes' or 'Wardrobes' because the engine doors of the locomotive are on the body side. This name was sometimes also applied to the Class 20s.

Another photograph taken at Water Orton, this time on 6 May 1987 showing Class 58 No. 58043 heading for the Birmingham area with a coal train from the Leicester direction. Water Orton is also the junction for the line to Derby, which can be seen on the left. In the misty distance is Hams Hall power station, which has since been demolished, the area now being a freight terminal.

The Class 58s were the first locomotives to appear in the Railfreight grey livery.

We complete this quartet of coal trains with a photograph taken at the north end of Leicester London Road station on 15 June 1983. Passing Leicester North signal-box and approaching the camera is Class 45/1 No. 45114 with a southbound coal train. On the far right can be seen the edge of Leicester diesel depot. This is on the site of the old Leicester (Midland) steam shed, which was numbered 15C.

These four scenes show branch lines that were active in the 1980s.

Left: The first photograph was taken on 17 April 1984 and shows Class 47 No. 47291 on the Redmire branch, just east of Leyburn, with a Redmire to Tees Yard hopper train. (See also page 57.)

Below left: The second scene shows Class 25/2 No. 25239 shunting vans at Warcop station on the branch line from Appleby on 30 September 1983. This line was originally part of the North Eastern line from the WCML at Eden Valley Junction to Kirkby Stephen and the north-east of England.

Opposite top: This photograph was taken at Newton-on-Ayr on 18 August 1983 and shows Class 20 locomotives Nos 20213 and 20011 as they climb up the Ayr Harbour branch and approach the Ayr to Glasgow main line (front right) with empty coal wagons for the Ayrshire coalfields. Note the G&SWR Ayr Harbour Junction signal-box.

Opposite below: The final scene is on the Newquay branch and shows Class 08 No. 08945 as it approaches St Blazey with a short freight train from Goonbarrow on 27 April 1984.

The old tented china clay wagons (which finished work in 1987) were, in my opinion, very photogenic, probably because they date back to GWR days. On 9 August 1984 Class 37s Nos 37185 and 37273 run through the four-track section of Totnes station and head west with a train of tented wagons, probably from the Heathfield branch (near Newton Abbot) to St Blazey. On the left is the edge of Totnes signal-box, by then out of use but today known as the excellent Signal-Box Café, and on the right hanging flower baskets and a GWR hand trolley.

The second view *(below)* shows Class 37 No. 37176 as it runs down to Lostwithiel on 27 April 1984 with a load of china clay wagons from Carne Point on the old Fowey branch, the junction being just behind the train. The locomotive will then shunt the wagons into the sidings at Lostwithiel station.

On 27 April 1984 the annual weed-killing train pauses at Par station, having just been at work on the Newquay line, with Class 37 No. 37182 in charge. A few minutes later the 09.33 Penzance to Paddington HST service arrived at Par and was in trouble, so the Class 37 was taken off the weed-killing train, put on the front of the HST and then the 09.33 Up Penzance left for Plymouth.

Class 37/5 No. 37673 is highlighted by the autumn sunshine as it climbs the 1 in 47 of Rattery Bank to the west of Totnes with a smart midday freight train bound for Plymouth and St Blazey on 27 November 1987.

The final photograph in this section shows the Up evening postal train (19.22 ex-Penzance) near Marazion on the outskirts of Penzance, hauled by Class 47/4 No. 47524 on 17 August 1989. Sadly, this service finished in January 2004. The former GWR Marazion station house is shown still in situ, surrounded by the famous camping coaches, but these have now all gone. Completing the scene is Mounts Bay.

Chapter Seven

City Stations

There is surely no better place to start a section on city stations than the former North Eastern station at York. On 23 May 1981 a Peak Class 45 locomotive leaves York station with an afternoon York to Liverpool train. Note the NER metal scroll sign on the pillar, far right.

These four photographs at Exeter St Davids demonstrate what it was like to visit a large busy station in the 1980s, with a wide variety of locomotives, a good display of semaphore signals and signal-boxes and plenty of action to see. Unlike York station (see previous page), this ex-GWR station has fine GWR canopies over its platforms rather than an overall roof. *Above:* Class 47 No. 47131 eases down the 1 in 37 between Exeter Central and St Davids on 28 April 1984 with the 09.10 Waterloo to Exeter service. The train is just crossing the main line to Plymouth and above the second coach is Exeter West signal-box. *Below:* On the same day, Class 08 No. 08840 pauses between shunting duties. In the background is the new power box which will be in use by the following year, thus ending semaphore signalling in the Exeter area. This photograph also illustrates the GWR canopies.

This view shows Class 45/1 No. 45150 ready to leave Exeter St Davids with the 07.40 Penzance to Liverpool Lime Street train on 28 April 1984. The crossing keeper is on the level crossing, and the train is signalled. Under the gantry can be seen Exeter North box which controls this area and also, at the bottom of the box, is the crossing keeper's hut. In the distance is a fine array of semaphore signals.

The fourth photograph at Exeter St Davids was taken on 28 August 1984. Class 50 No. 50008 *Thunderer* waits to pull out with the 09.32 Penzance to Paddington train.

In pre-grouping days, Carlisle station played host to many railway companies, and a wide range of steam locomotives. It was obviously not the same in the 1980s, but there was still a variety of traction to be seen. *Opposite:* Class 25 No. 25064 pauses light-engine in the station on 22 April 1984, framed by a stone archway from pre-grouping days. *Above:* The following day (23 April 1984) sees Class 40 No. 40104 waiting to leave the station loop line with a southbound mineral train, while in platform 1 is a Class 81 electric locomotive with a southbound WCML extra. These Class 81 locomotives were first introduced in 1959 for use on the West Coast Main Line.

The third photograph at Carlisle was taken at 16.19, also on 23 April 1984, and shows the 13.50 from Glasgow Central (routed via Kilmarnock and Annan) arriving behind Class 26 No. 26037. Overlooking the scene is a fine array of Victorian architecture. Notice the lattice work on the road overbridge.

Newcastle Central station on the ECML is our next location. The photographs opposite and right were taken on 11 August 1986, the year before the electrification of the Newcastle area.
Opposite top: Class 31/4 No. 31435 waits to leave Newcastle Central station with a southbound afternoon parcels train. *Opposite below*: Class 03 shunter No. 03078 pauses in one of Central's bay platforms during shunting duties. These shunting engines were first introduced in 1957. They were built by BR Swindon or Doncaster works and were withdrawn from BR by the end of the 1980s. Many examples found employment in private industry and several have been preserved. *Right*: The third view is of the east end of Newcastle Central station, taken from the castle keep. HST No. 43061 is seen leaving the vast station with the 10.30 Kings Cross to Edinburgh service. Some of the outer platforms have gone to make way for car parking, and there are already signs of trackside work in readiness for electrification. But the famous diamond crossing can still be clearly seen.

Class 31/4 No. 31424 pulls out of Norwich Thorpe station on 6 August 1983 with the 09.35 to Birmingham New Street train. Stabled on the left is Class 37 No. 37110, and in the background is a Class 47 on the 09.40 Liverpool Street train. Notice the abundance of semaphore signals. With electrification of the Liverpool Street to Norwich line by the mid-1980s, scenes like this would change dramatically.

We are now at York station where the first scene *(above)*, taken on 9 July 1986, shows on the right Class 45/1 No. 45103 just arrived with the 09.03 Liverpool Lime Street to Scarborough train, while on the left is No. 45144 which, after removal of No. 45103, will take the train forward to Scarborough. Since this photograph was taken, and with electrification, the centre through roads have been removed. *Below*: Taken two years later, on 4 September 1988, this photograph shows Class 47/4 No. 47551 at the south end of York station, on the 11.03 Newcastle to Poole train. The view well illustrates the attractive canopies and fine overall roof. *Opposite*: This scene at York was photographed from the station footbridge, and shows Class 45/1 No. 45105 at York station with the 08.03 Liverpool to Newcastle train on 27 July 1986.

Class 47/4 No. 47622 pauses at Worcester Shrub Hill station on Sunday 19 April 1987 with the 16.15 Hereford to Paddington train. This fine old station originally had an overall roof, and was a GWR/MR joint station. In steam days there was a fairly large steam depot (85A) with two engine sheds and also a locomotive works, the shed and the works being at the northern end of the station. The diesel stabling depot, which is on the site of the steam shed, can be seen under the station footbridge. Note on the right the extensive goods sidings. Also, behind the photographer were other goods sidings, which were known as the Midland yard.

One of Brunel's masterpieces, Bristol Temple Meads station, is our next setting. Photographed beneath its splendid roof on 2 June 1983 is an HST unit on an afternoon train to South Wales, while on the left-hand side is Class 31 No. 31102 on an empty stock train. A comparison with the top picture on page 96 will show different front end roofs, No. 31102 being one of a batch of Class 31s built without a panel on the front end roof.

Framed by a road overbridge at the eastern end of Manchester Victoria station, Class 40 No. 40057 is seen with the ECS train for the 15.15 service to Bangor on 29 January 1983. The train is coming in from Red Bank carriage sidings, situated around a mile from the station on the line to Bury. On the right, a DMU is approaching Victoria station with a local service, while on the left can be seen Class 46 No. 46037 and Class 08 No. 08675.

The Class 46s were a final development of the Peak Class 45, and were first introduced in 1961.

This second view at Bristol was taken at the western end of Temple Meads station, and shows English Electric Class 50 No. 50016 *Barham* departing with the 16.15 train to Taunton via Weston-super-Mare on 2 June 1983.

The nickname for the Class 50s among enthusiasts is 'Hoover'. This is because of the sound that they make – reputed to be the loudest in BR's diesel fleet.

The rear of an afternoon Edinburgh to Glasgow push-and-pull shuttle train enters The Mound Tunnel, just to the west of Edinburgh Waverley station, on 11 May 1983. The traction is provided by Class 47/7 No. 47706 *Strathclyde*, one of a group of Class 47s modified for push-and-pull operation.

Edinburgh Waverley station on a sunny 30 March 1986 sees Class 47/4 No. 47408 leaving with the 13.20 train to Dundee. Note the fine platform canopies and road overbridge. Overlooking the scene is the North British Hotel, complete with elegant clock tower.

Chapter Eight
Seaside Days

Where better to start this chapter than at Britain's most famous seaside resort, Blackpool. On Saturday 17 September 1983 Class 47/4 No. 47447 waits to leave Blackpool North station with the 09.34 train to London Euston. In the background are a variety of DMUs on local services to Lancashire and Yorkshire cities and towns. The fine LMS bracket signal neatly frames the renowned Blackpool Tower.

Turning round from where the photograph on page 103 was taken, we see Class 47 No. 47014 entering
Blackpool North station, also on 17 September 1983, with the 07.10 train from Newcastle. Blackpool North No. 2
signal-box dates from Lancashire & Yorkshire (L&YR) days, and the semaphore signals are a mixture of LMS
and BR types.

Cleethorpes, on the Lincolnshire coast, may not be as famous as Blackpool, but in the 1980s it still possessed a fine array of LNER-type bracket signals, as can be seen in this view of Class 31/4 No. 31408 arriving at Cleethorpes station on 26 July 1983 with the 12.07 from Newark North Gate. Just above the train is the roof of the Great Central Railway (GCR) signal-box.

Another Lincolnshire seaside resort popular with holiday-makers and also railway enthusiasts is Skegness, where in the summer timetable of the 1980s, especially on summer Saturdays, a variety of motive power would be seen on trains to and from the Midlands, Lancashire and Yorkshire. Arguably the most popular were the pairs of Class 20s ('Choppers') which ran on some summer weekdays as well as Saturdays between the East Midlands and Skegness. On Saturday 16 July 1983 Class 20s Nos 20187 and 20183 leave Skegness with the 12.37 to Leicester. The disc on the front of the train reads 'Group 20 Chopper Bash'. The signals on the left are a mixture of GNR (concrete post) and LNER (wooden post), both with more modern semaphore blades.

The ECML around the Berwick-upon-Tweed area, certainly until the electrification of the line in 1987, provided not only the rail traveller but also the railway photographer with many fine sea views. On 1 August 1987 (just prior to electrification) the 14.35 Edinburgh to Kings Cross HST service runs by Lamberton beach, just north of Berwick-upon-Tweed. In the background, right, is the North Sea. The leading power car is No. 43045 *The Grammar School Doncaster AD 1350*, with No. 43073 at the rear.

On Sunday 14 July 1985 Class 45/1 No. 45122 speeds by the harbour at Cockwood, near Starcross, with the 14.55 Plymouth to Birmingham New Street train. *(Christina Siviter)*

The Exmouth to Paignton service is only a local train, but it runs through some fine scenery. On 15 August 1987 the 15.15 train, comprising two Class 142 'Skipper' units in GWR chocolate and cream livery, with No. 142021 leading, runs through Horse (or Shell) Cove on its journey to the Torbay resort of Paignton. In the background is the seaside town of Dawlish. These units were introduced in 1985, but had only a short stay in the south-west.

We complete this quartet of seascapes with a view of the spectacular sea wall at Teignmouth. On 12 April 1983 Class 45/1 No. 45143 *5th Royal Inniskilling Dragoon Guards* approaches the camera with the 11.58 Paignton to Exeter train. Disappearing into the distance towards Teignmouth station is a morning Paddington to Plymouth HST service.

The Yorkshire seaside town of Whitby, famous as the home of Captain James Cook and also of the great Victorian photographer Frank Meadow Sutcliffe, is our next location. A Metropolitan-Cammell Class 101 two-car DMU waits to leave the attractive stone-built station on 17 April 1984 with the 16.10 service to Darlington. The scene is overlooked by some fine Victorian houses.

Probably the most famous of all the Yorkshire seaside resorts is Scarborough. On 14 August 1983 Class 45/1 No. 45129 passes under the LNER gantry signal next to Falsgrave signal-box as it leaves Scarborough with the 14.25 train to Liverpool.

Another view of Scarborough on 14 August 1983, only this time showing the station. Class 47 No. 47212 waits to leave with the 11.00 train to Leeds, while on the right Class 08 No. 08339 shunts empty coaching stock. A splendid gantry signal controls the station movements. In the 1980s it seemed as if the seaside stations always managed to retain their lovely old semaphore signals, when nearly everywhere else they were disappearing.

A famous push-and-pull service in the 1980s was that between Waterloo and Weymouth, with nineteen members of the Class 33 locomotives (Nos 33101 to 33119) being modified for the purpose and classed 33/1. The early evening of 29 August 1983 sees the rear of the 17.20 Weymouth to Waterloo service as it leaves the Dorset seaside resort and port with Class 33 No. 33118 at the back of the train. Dominating the scene is the ex-Southern Railway rail-built signal, complete with raised disc signals; notice the stylish finials.

The North Wales coast between Prestatyn and Llandudno has always been a popular area, especially for caravan holidays. Class 47/4 No. 47549 enters Abergele & Pensarn station on 4 June 1983 with the 15.37 Crewe to Holyhead train. This photograph was taken from the signal-box by kind permission of BR. On the right is the large caravan park at Abergele, and on the left the Irish Sea, with a footbridge linking the two.

The resort of Llandudno is served by a short branch line (3 miles in length) off the North Wales main line at Llandudno Junction. In the 1980s there were through workings by locomotive-hauled trains from Crewe for the Midlands and London, and also from Manchester and the north-east. On 18 June 1983 Class 47/4 No. 47563 pulls away from Llandudno station with the 18.00 to Crewe. As at Abergele *(top)* there is still a fair number of semaphore signals.

Class 50 No. 50047 *Swiftsure* is framed by the station footbridge as it approaches Dawlish on Saturday 30 July 1983 with the 14.45 Paignton to Paddington train. Although No. 50047, along with the rest of the class, had been refurbished, it was (with certain other members of the class) repainted in the old BR blue livery.

Sporting the new livery (after refurbishment), Class 50 No. 50030 *Repulse* pulls away from the former GWR station at Paignton with the 11.45 train to Paddington on Saturday 1 September 1984.

This busy scene was photographed at Penzance early on the morning of 17 August 1984. In the foreground, Class 50 No. 50002 *Superb* waits to leave with the 07.30 train to Glasgow, which is scheduled to arrive at 18.47. Behind No. 50002 is Class 47 No. 47145 on the empty stock of the 08.53 train to Newcastle. In the sidings are a pair of Class 50s, on the right No. 50005 *Collingwood* and No. 50011 *Centurion*, and just visible behind these two locomotives is Class 45/1 No. 45126. In the harbour is the *Scillonian*, which sails between Penzance and the Scilly Isles.

A little later on the same day we see Class 50 No. 50005 pulling out of Brunel's fine terminus at Penzance with the 09.32 to Paddington. On the left is Class 47/4 No. 47567.

We conclude this set of seaside photographs with another view at Skegness, taken on 16 July 1983. Class 37 No. 37196 is seen arriving at Skegness station with the 08.18 train from Manchester Piccadilly. On the right is the Great Northern signal-box, and the bracket signals are of BR design.

Chapter Nine
Peaks on the Midland

From the early 1960s until the summer timetable of 1983 the Peak Class 45 locomotives held sway on the Midland main line passenger trains between St Pancras and Leicester, Derby, Nottingham and Sheffield. And so it would have been no surprise to see three members of this class at St Pancras station on Saturday 20 June 1981. On the right, No. 45132 has just arrived with a midday departure from Leicester. In the centre is light engine No. 45118 *The Royal Artilleryman*, and on the left is an unidentified member of the class on an empty stock train.

On the final Saturday of the 1982/83 winter timetable, 14 May 1983, Class 45/1 No. 45149 sweeps round the curves to the south of Wellingborough station with the 14.05 St Pancras to Nottingham train. Note the high semaphore signal for sighting purposes.

On 20 April 1983 No. 45125 leaves Market Harborough station with a morning Leicester to London (St Pancras) train. Note the semaphore signals; these would disappear by 1987 with resignalling in the area.

One of the most interesting locations in the Wellingborough area, from a railway point of view, was the goods yard at Finedon Road, just to the north of Wellingborough station. On the last day of their regular working on this route, 15 May 1983, Class 45/1 No. 45128 (with split headcode) makes a fine sight as it runs past Finedon Road signal-box with an early evening train from Sheffield to St Pancras. In the background is the extensive goods yard, with a fair amount of traffic in it. Note also the wooden-post signals, a nice reminder of the Midland Railway.

The photographs on this page and opposite, top, were taken at Kettering (for Corby) station on 20 April 1983. *Above*: Class 45/1 No. 45103 heads north with a midday St Pancras to Nottingham train. Note the double-pole telegraph poles. *Below*: No. 45111 *Grenadier Guardsman* leans into the curves as it speeds south with an Up London train. Both these scenes give good views of the Midland Railway signal-box.

The third view of Kettering photographed on 20 April 1983 shows No. 45111 as it runs into the station with the Up London train seen in the previous picture. The splendid architecture is worthy of note.

Loughborough is another fine Midland station. On 12 June 1982 Class 45/1 No. 45104 *The Royal Warwickshire Fusiliers* enters the station with a morning St Pancras to Nottingham train. Next to the station, off the left-hand side of the photograph, is the home of Brush Traction, the builder of many of the locomotives featured in this book, in particular the Type 4 Class 47s and Type 2 Class 31s.

This wider view of St Pancras station was taken on 20 June 1981, the same day as the photograph on page 115, and shows in full No. 45118 *The Royal Artilleryman* after arrival in the early afternoon on a train from Sheffield. This light and airy Victorian station with its splendid roof was opened in 1868. The famous gasholder can be seen dimly at the rear of the train.

Although much of their work on the Midland main line had ceased after 15 May 1983, the Class 45s that were left, many having been transferred to work on the North Wales main line, were often used on more mundane duties. At Leicester London Road station on 9 July 1983 Class 45 No. 45052 is seen about to shunt the empty stock of the 12.37 Skegness to Leicester train, which had earlier arrived behind Class 20s Nos 20183 and 20187.

Framed by a variety of semaphore signals, an unidentified Class 45 approaches Wellingborough with a St Pancras to Chesterfield special charter train on 14 May 1983.

Class 45/1 No. 45132 heads out of Wellingborough just after 9 a.m. on Saturday 14 May 1983 and approaches Finedon Road goods yard with a northbound express. In the background, one of the old steam sheds (15A) can be seen clearly, to the left of which is the diesel depot. This was built on the site of the other steam shed which had been demolished in 1964.

The final scene in this chapter was photographed on Sunday 15 May 1983 (the last day of the winter timetable), and shows Class 45/1 No. 45114 leaving Wellingborough station with the 16.50 St Pancras to Sheffield train. From the following day the Class 45 passenger duties on this route, apart from breakdowns, would be mainly in the hands of HST units. Note the lovely old MR signal-box and fine mixture of semaphore signals, chiefly of LMS origin.

Chapter Ten
Stations & Junctions

A busy scene at Westbury on 26 May 1983. Class 33 No. 33026 pulls out of one of the station's four platforms with the 11.10 Portsmouth Harbour to Bristol Temple Meads train. On the right, Class 47 No. 47069 is seen shunting a tank train, at the rear of which the diesel depot is just visible. Complementing the GWR signal-box is a fine array of GWR semaphore signals, all of which would be shortly making way for colour light signalling when the new power box came into operation (see top photograph on page 65).

The branch line from Marks Tey (just south of Colchester on the main line to London Liverpool Street station) to Sudbury was originally part of the Great Eastern line from Colchester to Cambridge and also north to Bury St Edmunds and Thetford, the junction for these two routes being at Long Melford, just to the north of Sudbury. These lines closed many years ago, leaving the 11 miles between Marks Tey and Sudbury as a reminder of these cross-country routes. On 5 August 1983 the driver of the 13.35 service to Colchester telephones control for permission to leave the branch terminus at Sudbury. The train comprises a Class 105 Craven two-car DMU No. E51478, which was built in 1959. Although the station has seen better days, the Great Eastern Railway (GER) station building, complete with a platform canopy, still looks in reasonable order, and the northbound platform is still in situ.

Another GER station, this time at Brundall Junction on the Norwich to Yarmouth/Lowestoft routes. Class 31 No. 31261 pulls away from the eastbound staggered platform with the 11.28 Norwich to Yarmouth train on 6 August 1983. Note the GER footbridge, and high semaphore signals for sighting purposes.

It is around 5.30 p.m. on Friday 5 August 1983, and the driver of the 16.20 Liverpool Street to Norwich, 'The East Anglian', takes advantage of the two-minute stop at Ipswich to chat to a colleague. The immaculate Class 47/4 locomotive is No. 47580 *The County of Essex*, which is shedded at Stratford depot. Above the train can be seen the lovely station canopies of this fine example of a Great Eastern station. Note also the train's headboard, a rather rare practice in the 1980s.

The 13.05 Weymouth to Bristol train, comprising Pressed Steel Co. Class 117 three-car DMU No. B438 built in 1959, enters the attractive junction station of Castle Cary on 29 August 1983 to find a fair number of passengers waiting to board it. The station buildings still look in good order, as does the old goods shed, although not now in railway use. At this time there were still semaphore signals and an unusual signal-box, but as can be seen from the crosses these were shortly due to be replaced with the resignalling in the area. The single line to Yeovil Pen Mill and Weymouth can be seen going away to the left, with the ex-GWR West of England main line to Taunton swinging away to the right. Note also the route indicator on the GWR backing signal, just above the train.

One of the most attractive ex-GWR junction stations is at Par (on the Plymouth to Penzance main line), which is the junction for the line to St Blazey and on to the seaside resort of Newquay. On the late afternoon of 31 August 1984 Class 37 No. 37181 and Class 47 No. 47105 head through Par with a freight from St Blazey to the Stoke-on-Trent area. The line to St Blazey and Newquay is on the right-hand side at the rear of the train. In the background are the chimneys of the clay drying plant at Par Docks (ECC).

Sadly Seaton Junction is not a junction station any more, for the branch line to Seaton from here was closed in March 1966. However, to all railway enthusiasts I am sure it will always be known as Seaton Junction. On 19 February 1985 Class 50 No. 50001 *Dreadnought* is seen speeding through the remains of the junction station with the 14.17 Exeter to Waterloo train. On the right is an old loading gauge, and on the extreme left (coming towards the photographer) is the trackbed of the start of the branch line. The Up station building is still in private commercial use. As can be seen, there were originally four tracks through the station, which gives some idea of how busy this junction station once was.

Although Tiverton Junction had lost its two branch lines, the one to Tiverton in 1964 and the branch to Hemyock in 1975, the station itself remained open until 9 May 1986. It was replaced by Tiverton Parkway, a mile or so to the north of the old junction station. On 7 May 1985 the 08.53 Penzance to Newcastle train, with Class 50 No. 50017 *Royal Oak* in charge, is seen heading through Tiverton Junction station on its journey to the north-east. On the right is the last remnant of track of the Hemyock branch, and on the left is the Esso oil terminal; completing the scene is a good display of GWR semaphore signals.

These two photographs were taken on Saturday 13 August 1983 in mid-Wales at Dovey Junction, where the line from Shrewsbury divides, with one route running north to Barmouth and Pwllheli, and the other running south to Aberystwyth. The first view *(above)* shows a pair of Class 25s, Nos 25181 and 25229, as they enter the Aberystwyth platform at Dovey Junction with the (SO) 10.10 Aberystwyth to Wolverhampton train. In the second photograph *(below)*, we see a Metropolitan-Cammell Class 101 three-car DMU with the 09.21 Shrewsbury to Pwllheli service entering the Barmouth side of the junction station. The Cambrian Hills provide an attractive backdrop. Notice the fine array of GWR semaphore signals, some with route indicators.

Another attractive station on the Cambrian line is at Caersws, situated between Newtown and Carno. On 26 May 1987 this former junction station for the branch line to Garth Road and Van (which closed in 1940) plays host to the 09.40 Pwllheli to Shrewsbury (and Wolverhampton), which comprised one of the (then) new Class 150 DMUs, No. 150140. These were first introduced in 1984, and were built at BREL York works. The station crossing gates are still worked by hand, and the signal-box and station building are also worthy of note, but the loop line has by this time been truncated.

Sutton Bridge Junction, just south of Shrewsbury station, is where the Cambrian line to Welshpool and beyond leaves the Shrewsbury–Hereford–Newport route. On Saturday 10 June 1989 Class 37/4 No. 37430 *Cwmbrân* and No. 37429 *Eisteddfod Genedlaethol* leave the Cambrian line at Sutton Bridge Junction and head for Shrewsbury with the 10.13 Aberystwyth to Euston train, which was, as usual, loaded up to twelve coaches.

Newton Abbot station, with its spacious platforms, attractive station buildings, and an abundance of trackwork and semaphore signals, is the setting as Class 50 No. 50040 *Leviathan* pulls out of platform 1 with the (SO) 07.00 Oxford to Paignton train on 7 September 1985. Within two years this scene would alter radically, with semaphores being changed for colour light signalling, just three lines through the station remaining, the goods lines being taken out and the platforms being shortened.

On 28 August 1985 Class 47/4 No. 47606 with the 15.20 Plymouth to Paddington train pulls through Newbury station just as Class 50 No. 50046 *Ajax* pulls away from platform 1 with an empty stock train bound for Paddington, having earlier arrived with the 16.45 Paddington to Newbury train.

On Sunday 12 June 1983 Class 33 No. 33062 approaches Severn Tunnel Junction station with the 11.10 Cardiff to Portsmouth Harbour service. The popular Type 3 'Cromptons' were regular performers on this route until the summer timetable of 1988. Note the diesel depot behind the train with Classes 08, 25, 31, 37 and 47 on display. The junction for the line to Gloucester is just east of the station.

At Hove, on 30 August 1983, a Class 73 electro-diesel No. 73109 waits to leave the station with a pick-up goods for the London area. The nickname for these locomotives is 'Eds'.

In December 1985 I was playing trumpet with the Syd Lawrence Orchestra, including a one-night stand at Carmarthen (Trinity College) in West Wales. The following night we were playing at the Guildhall, Plymouth, and so after staying overnight at a hotel in Carmarthen, I was able to get down to the station in order to see one of the – by then – few loco-hauled trains in the area. Class 47/4 No. 47575 will shortly be leaving Carmarthen station with the 07.45 ex-Cardiff going forward as the 09.49 Carmarthen to Milford Haven on 20 December 1985. Note the BR uniforms of the 1980s.

Another winter scene, this time several hundred miles north of Carmarthen, at Huddersfield, West Yorkshire. The snow is settling as Class 45/1 No. 45106 prepares to leave the spacious station at 1.39 p.m. with the 11.20 Newcastle to Liverpool Lime Street train on 21 February 1986. This station, which was first opened in 1847, possesses what is probably the most attractive station façade in England. It was threatened by demolition in the 1960s, but thankfully was bought by Huddersfield Corporation in 1968 and restored to its former glory.

Several NER stations in the north-east of England had fine-looking overall roofs, including the one at the famous railway town of Darlington. On 13 August 1986 Class 45/1 No. 45112 *The Royal Army Ordnance Corps* waits to leave Darlington with the 08.03 Liverpool to Newcastle train. For many years, until their withdrawal from service in about 1987, the Peak Class locomotives were regular performers on the northern cross-country trains.

On 7 May 1984 Class 33 No. 33030 heads past Clink Road Junction near Frome with an Up ECS train bound for Westbury. The line from the junction runs through to Frome station and then back onto the former GWR West of England main line at Blatchbridge Junction, the section of main line between the two junctions being known as the 'Frome Cut-Off'. Also just before Frome station is the junction for the line to the ARC Whatley quarry, this being part of the GWR line to Radstock and on to Bristol, which closed in the 1960s. Note the GWR signal-box of wooden construction.

Before the reopening in 1995 of the former GWR route from Birmingham to Stourbridge Junction (the new Birmingham Snow Hill station had opened in 1987), trains to Stourbridge Junction and Kidderminster from Birmingham had used New Street station, gaining access to the former GWR route at Galton Junction, just to the east of Smethwick West. On 23 November 1983 a Derby-built Class 116 three-car DMU approaches the former GWR signal-box at Smethwick West with the 10.15 New Street to Stourbridge Junction train. In the foreground is the truncated GWR line to Handsworth Junction on the GWR Snow Hill to Wolverhampton line. This route from Snow Hill to Wolverhampton closed in 1972, but today the trackbed of this former line is used by a rapid transit tram system from Snow Hill to Wolverhampton.

Class 45/1 No. 45125 climbs Miles Platting Bank, north-east of Manchester Victoria station, and approaches Miles Platting Junction with the 12.05 Liverpool to Scarborough train on 27 June 1984. In a few yards the train will take the line to Stalybridge and Huddersfield (via the Diggle route), the line straight ahead of the train running to Rochdale and Todmorden. A glance at the rear of the train gives some idea of the steepness of Miles Platting Bank, which is some 2,320yd long, and 1 in 47 at its steepest. In steam days banking locomotives would wait at Manchester Victoria station to assist the heavier trains up this incline.

On 15 April 1984 Class 37 No. 37096 heads past Hellifield South signal-box and takes the line to Blackburn and Preston with the 12.05 Carlisle to Preston ECS train. To the right of the train is the line running to Skipton and Leeds.

Our next location is Helsby Junction on the Manchester to Chester main line. This attractive station is the junction for the line to Ellesmere Port and Hooton (on the Chester to Liverpool line). On 14 April 1983 a smart Class 25 No. 25044 heads towards Manchester with an inspection train from Hooton. In the branch platform are a pair of Class 114 units forming a local service to Ellesmere Port and Hooton. Note the high repeating signals and station signal-box (to the left of the DMU) as well as the ornate pre-grouping station buildings, complete with a fine array of chimneys.

No chapter on stations and junctions would be complete without a view of the most northerly junction in the UK at Georgemas, junction station for Thurso to the north and Wick to the east. This picture of Georgemas Junction was taken on Sunday 24 July 1988, and shows Class 37/4 No. 37421 having just arrived with the 11.22 from Thurso, then shunting the stock onto the 11.20 from Wick, which will then form the 11.46 to Inverness, hauled by Class 37/4 No. 37414. The line to Thurso can be clearly seen swinging away under the splendid Highland Railway footbridge. By the summer timetable of 1989 Sprinter units had taken over these services.

Chapter Eleven
Night Scenes

The first photograph in this final chapter is something of an anachronism, because by the time this picture had been taken, on the evening of Friday 20 September 1985, the popular Class 52 Western hydraulic diesels had long been withdrawn, in 1977 in fact. I was visiting Landor depot at Swansea late that evening to take a picture of the GWR Castle Class 4–6–0 No. 5051 *Drysllwyn Castle*, which during that weekend was due to work on the Swansea to Carmarthen steam charter trains run in connection with the GWR 150 celebrations. To my pleasure I found Class 52 No. D1062 *Western Courier* undergoing work in the depot. This locomotive is owned by the Western Locomotive Association, and is now based on the Severn Valley Railway.

I was standing in the concourse of Blackpool North station at around 9 p.m. on Friday 16 September 1983, when I heard a high-pitched whistling sound coming from inside the station. On investigating the sound, I was very pleased to see Class 40 ('Whistler') No. 40155 at rest in platform 3 after bringing in a train from Euston, the Class 40 having come on the train at Preston.

A winter's night at Worcester Shrub Hill station (5 January 1984) as Class 47/4 No. 47482 pauses after arriving at platform 2 with the 17.07 Paddington to Hereford train.

On the evening of 21 October 1981 Class 45 No. 45019 waits to leave York station with a postal train bound for Bristol. The classic lines of the station's overall roof can be seen above the platform canopies.

In the early to mid-1980s the Class 33 'Crompton' locomotives were often found on passenger trains in the south-west. The evening of 31 October 1984 sees Class 33 No. 33004 at platform 3 of Newton Abbot station with the 18.35 stopping train from Paignton to Cardiff Central station, with arrival in the Welsh capital city at 22.12.

At large stations locomotives are often stabled on the through lines, as was the case at Carlisle Citadel station on the evening of 29 January 1983. A smart Class 08 shunter No. 08844 is seen waiting to move Class 81 electric locomotive No. 81008.

The Class 81s were built between 1960 and 1961 by the Birmingham RC&W Co. at its Smethwick works, for use on the newly electrified (at the time) WCML between London, Birmingham, Manchester, Liverpool, the far north-west and then on to Glasgow. They were withdrawn from service by the early 1990s. One example is preserved, No. E3003 (No. 81002), by the A/C Locomotive Group at Barrow Hill Roundhouse, Chesterfield.

Although the Class 45 locomotives had finished on regular passenger service on the Midland main line out of St Pancras in May 1983, even in 1985 they could be found at the former Midland Railway's London terminus on other duties. On 25 March 1985 the splendid station clock at St Pancras tells us it is 7.16 p.m., and Class 45/1 No. 45122 is already at the head of the postal train to Newcastle, although it is not due to leave until 10.25 p.m.

Class 50 No. 50011 *Centurion* waits under the roof of Brunel's terminus station at Penzance on the evening of 28 August 1984. Shortly it will be joined by No. 50017 *Royal Oak*. Both locomotives will run forward and then back onto the night sleeper train to Paddington, which will depart from Penzance at 21.35.

Birmingham New Street in daylight has never been regarded as a very photogenic station, but at night it certainly is, as these two photographs, taken on 24 January 1983, testify.
Above: This view shows Pressed Steel Co. Class 117 three-car DMU No. 51370 on a local train to Worcester. These units were first introduced in 1959.
Left: A Class 108 three-car DMU pausing in one of this large station's centre roads.

A wet night at Plymouth North Road station on 2 April 1985 as Class 50 No. 50018 *Resolution* waits for the arrival of the 07.30 Aberdeen to Penzance train (which was brought in by No. 50045 *Achilles*). No. 50045 will then come off the train, which will be taken forward to Penzance by No. 50018.

Class 08 shunter No. 08910 pauses between shunting duties during a very wet night on 29 January 1983 at Carlisle Citadel station.

Bibliography

Heavyside, Tom, *Tribute to the Deltics*, David & Charles, 1982
Morrison, Brian, *BR Traction in Colour*, Ian Allan, 1987
Siviter, Roger, *Diesels and Semaphores*, OPC, 1985
——, *50s to Exeter*, Silver Link, 1992
——, *Scotland East & North*, Great Bear Publishing, 2003
——, *Taunton West*, Great Bear Publishing, 2004
——, *The Wash to Worcester*, Great Bear Publishing, 2005
——, *50s in Devon & Cornwall*, Kingfisher/Runpast, 1989
——, *37s in the Highlands*, Kingfisher/Runpast, 1989
——, *50s West*, Great Bear Publishing, 2001
——, *Waterloo West*, Great Bear Publishing, 2002
Vaughan, John, *Diesels in the Duchy*, Ian Allan, 1983
Traction magazine
Railway magazine

This final photograph shows English Electric Class 50 No. 50005 *Collingwood* stabled at Penzance on the evening of 16 August 1984. In the background is the *Scillonian*.